The Night of the Wild Horses

GREGORY HARRISON

The Night of the Wild Horses

ILLUSTRATED BY VICTOR G. AMBRUS

London
OXFORD UNIVERSITY PRESS
1971

Oxford University Press, Ely House, London W.1

GLASGOW NEW YORK TORONTO MELBOURNE WELLINGTON
CAPE TOWN SALISBURY IBADAN NAIROBI DAR ES SALAAM LUSAKA
ADDIS ABABA BOMBAY CALCUTTA MADRAS KARACHI LAHORE
DACCA KUALA LUMPUR SINGAPORE HONG KONG TOKYO

© Gregory Harrison 1971
First published 1971

ISBN 0 19 276041 6

FOR
Gavin

PRINTED IN GREAT BRITAIN
BY W & J MACKAY & CO LTD, CHATHAM

Contents

MIDSUMMER NIGHT   1

I VISIT THE QUEEN   2

HEDGEHOG   3

A FAT OLD FARMER   6

FIRBY HALL   7

WATCHING THE TRAINS   8

THE SAILOR   13

THE GARDEN   14

MRS. PRIM   16

TUMULUS   17

I MET AN OLD MAN IN THE LANE   18

AIRCRAFT WARNING LIGHT   20

THE DUSTBIN MEN   21

HAY IN WINTER   23

THE COACH   24

YELLOW CAT   26

THE WEATHERCOCK   27

HELICOPTER   28

THE FOREST   30

AUSTRALIAN VISITOR   32

AT A BEAR-BAITING   36

ALONE IN THE GRANGE   37

MISS TORRENT   39

PONY AND TRAP   40

RACING THE TRAIN   42

THE NIGHT OF THE WILD HORSES   43

Midsummer Night

Midsummer Night,
And slowly shrinks the light
From lonely wolds;
The soft warm air of day
Still has not flowed away,
But washes the grassy hollows in
The hilly folds;
And in the shallow ditch,
Leaning on rampart slope,
Three soldiers wait and watch,
And listen, very still,
In the old stronghold on the hill.
They were not there two days ago,
Tomorrow will be gone,
But on this brief midsummer night
I do not stand alone.

I Visit the Queen

Ferdinand, Ferdinand,
Where have you been?
I've been up to London to look at the queen.
I've been with two horses,
A black and a grey;
They ate fifteen bundles
Of sweet-smelling hay.
At Buckingham Palace I stopped at the gate
And explained to the sentry why I was late.
The railings were splendid in black and in gold
And I tied up the horses and walked in the cold
Across the wide courtyard; the steps were so broad,
And someone in frockcoat said, 'Ticket, my Lord?'
I felt in my pocket—I knew it was there—
Mixed up with dog biscuits, an apple and pear.
And I bowed to the queen, and would you believe,
I remembered to cover the hole in my sleeve.
The queen very graciously chose not to see
The string round my trousers, the tear at my knee.
Ferdinand, Ferdinand,
Where have you been?
I've been up to London to look at the queen.
Ferdinand, Ferdinand,
What did you there?
I knelt to the queen and she touched my grey hair.

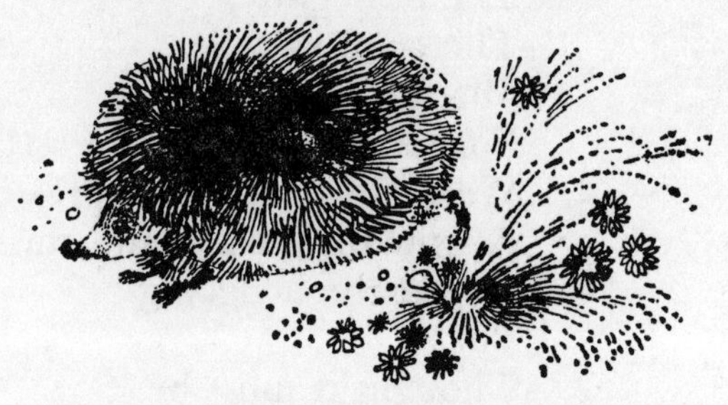

Hedgehog

It could have been a cat,
Tabby, wet,
Curled in with a mat
Of hair;
For the spines were soft and limp
And the animal was relaxed
And motionless. . . .

Until I coughed
It could have been dead,
But, no, it moved
Slowly pushing out
Its head
Through the long grass,
Questing,
With black nostrils at the tip
Of the long, pencil snout.

Not that the others,
The passers-by,
The country folk,
Shared
For a moment my interest;
Were not the least impressed.
A woman stopped and stared
Not at the hedgepig
But at me;
Thought it must be
Some sort of stunt,
And with a little grunt
Of impatience
Moved from the spot,
Her mind on toast,
A fire,
Tea steaming in the pot.

In her fawn raincoat
She moved on
Glad to be free;
Showed her contempt
Of animal and me
By how she limped
With shoulders thickly bent;
No malice meant—
Surprise and then indifference.

The hedgehog progressed towards the fence
Untroubled, without haste,
Lifting its back feet
Carefully and deliberately
As from soft toffee;
And the woman,

Thinking of tea,
Along the pavement paced
Lifting her low, black shoes
Deliberately,
Feet widely spaced
Under the fawn raincoat
Like a hedgehog's,
As from soft toffee.

Neither cared
For the other;
I, the spectator, stared.
I thought
As I lifted round my bike—
They were remarkably alike.

A Fat Old Farmer

A fat old farmer in the wolds
Was always catching dreadful colds;
He wrapped a stocking round his throat
And always wore an extra coat.
He sneezed and sneezed until his wife
Feared he would sneeze away his life.

She called to the hen-yard, 'Come, get into bed!'
He sneezed a great hole in the side of the shed.
She hurried downstairs and said, 'Lean on my arm.'
And he gave a great sneeze that shook the whole farm.
'Come get in the wagon. To the hospital, quick!'
And the hay filled the lane from a sneeze-flattened rick.
The horse turned its head, took one look at the face,
And tore down the lane at a furious pace.

So they sent for the doctor who said, 'He is ill.'
And he chose a bright scarlet, rectangular pill.
They laid him down gently and prepared to retreat,
And they opened his mouth and anchored his feet.
'Push it down,' yelled the doctor and the red pill got stuck.
The farmer got angry and quacked like a duck.
The pain was so sharp that he missed the next sneeze;
He shook off the doctor and crawled to his knees.
'I've got a sore throat. That pill's like a brick.'
'Yes,' the doctor agreed, 'it's my favourite trick.'

Firby Hall

From the yellow sandstone walls
Walk slowly down those steps,
So slow;
The heat strikes from the flags below
And I would have you stop
There,
Glowing in sunlight at the top,
For who can know
How soon this precious day will flow
Like water
Into long ago.
Walk slow
For I would hold you like a drop
Of water levelled in my hand,
And see you stand
For ever on those mossy stairs,
Nor move below
Out of the light;
The lawn a smell of autumn wears.

Watching the Trains

When grandad's pigeons were locked up
He'd sit astride his chair,
Rolling tobacco in his palms,
With lime-dust in his hair.

He'd tell me of the cinder wall,
The fat green stones like glass,
The crevices for dandelions,
The dusty, feathered grass;

Of steam-trains double-engined on
The gradient's skidding track,
Where a long clank of wagons lurched
Behind the fireman's back;

Of how he used to scrape his nails,
Scramble upon the wall
To watch the rattling monsters pant
Against the long slope's haul.

There was a tunnel on the line,
A bridge the scornful said;
A hundred yards of curving track
From arch to black arch led.

An agile lad could race a train
Hauling a heavy load
From where the flattened smoke
    squeezed in,
Across a busy road,

Across a traffic island,
Past a tobacco shop,
Beside some dusty dahlia beds
To the familiar top

Of look-out wall. Here he could wait
While cab in smoke-wrapped hood
Rumbled beneath pedestrians
To where my grandad stood.

By day grandad would dodge the cars,
Dash to the cinder wall
And hang above the tunnel mouth
In a precarious sprawl.

The thump and thunder pounded near,
The engine's smoky roar
Crashed from the dark hole underground,
A hellish, black guffaw.

       . . . . .

Two nights each week at ten to twelve
Dark in his bed he lay,
And heard the snuffle of the train
Muffled a mile away.

He'd hear it grinding up the slope,
The smoke slammed at the sky,
For every half-turn of the wheels,
A column steeple-high.

Then uncontrolled the slithering spin
Of driving-wheels burned fire,
Power flooded shuddering down the track
Beneath the iron tyre.

While other people moaned in sleep
Or sleepless cursed the train
The locomotive struggled near
Shaking the window-pane.

The trinkets on the dressing-stand,
The clock, the bedroom door
Rattled as if the engine crashed
Its smoke-box through the floor.

A cylinder of smoke rammed up
Mushroomed above the street;
The cold shock of linoleum
Twisted at grandad's feet.

For he must watch the fireman lunge
And thrust in blazing fight
To coal the monster straining through
The blackness of the night.

Each solid blast of the exhaust
Sucked at the window-pane;
The pistons' elbow-rods spun wheels
Greasy with drizzling rain.

And back in bed his feet kicked off
The chilly warming-pan;
Dark folded thickly in behind
The fiery caravan.

The wagons rattled on the gaps
And while the leader hauled
The second engine shoved behind
And slow past grandad crawled.

.   .   .   .   .

I know what grandad meant; I've seen
Just once a special train
With all the railway fans on board
Shuffling through the rain.

I ran, like grandad, to the arch;
The fire-box blasted red;
I would have sprawled across the wall
With grandad; but he's dead.

The Sailor

Johnnie's sat here
For a thousand year
Watching the ships slide down the stream,
For ships can glide
On the midday tide,
And the men can wave at sweetheart brave,
But boys can only dream.

Johnnie has dreamt for a thousand years
With the roar of breakers in his ears,
And his sailor's eye on the island palms
Where the white sands curve and gleam.
And one of these days from the look in his eyes
He'll do more than sit and dream and gaze;
He'll lean on the rail where the sun's ablaze
Under the tropic skies.

The Garden

I know a green and secret place
Where I can run or take my ease,
Where I can talk with birds and see
The stars peer at me through the trees.

It is my magic glade, a place
Where stags and badgers freely roam;
It is a forest where a hut
Provides me with a simple home.

It is a lonely mountain crag
Where buzzards wheel and eagles soar,
And in the deep ravine a stream
Bursts from the rocks with frothing roar.

It is the vast and heaving sea
Where albatross on giant wings
Circles my pitching ship and skims
The burnished dolphin as it springs.

Three classrooms and a timber-yard,
A tarmac playground and a wall,
These like an arm enclose and keep
A clearing where the blackbirds call.

I shall remember this green place,
The grass, the smell of earth, the tree,
The blossom falling and the sense
Of safety while being free.

It is my hiding-place, my fort,
My castle turreted and strong;
It is the place I go to find
Myself and my forgotten song.

Mrs. Prim

Mrs. Prim behind her curtains
Sees the world go by;
Nothing in the village happens
Unseen by her eye;
No word spoken in a cottage
Or in stately hall,
Tittle-tattle in the churchyard,
Gossip at the ball
Misses Mrs. Prim,
No fear—
All arrives in Madam's ear.
Vicar, postman, milkman, groom
Are her servants. Her front room
Throbs with conversation, news
Gathered both from pub and pews.

Mrs. Prim behind her curtains
Sniffs and gives a sigh,
Draws back very slightly
With a hard glint in her eye.
'I believe that's Mrs. Whatsit.
Who's the girl? Well, I declare;
Going in church with trousers on?
Oh no, she wouldn't dare!'

Tumulus

Lie quietly, revered and ancient king;
Do not torment your spirit with the ring
Of clinking plough that scatters earth and
    stones
And pares the dome above your foetal bones.

The plough-horse used to shy and rear,
Whinny aside from fearful mound;
And men would race the sinking sun
In pairs to scythe this rise of ground.

Today the scornful tractor tilts
A furrow through this holy place;
But ale-house ploughmen dare not still
Confront at night the regal face.

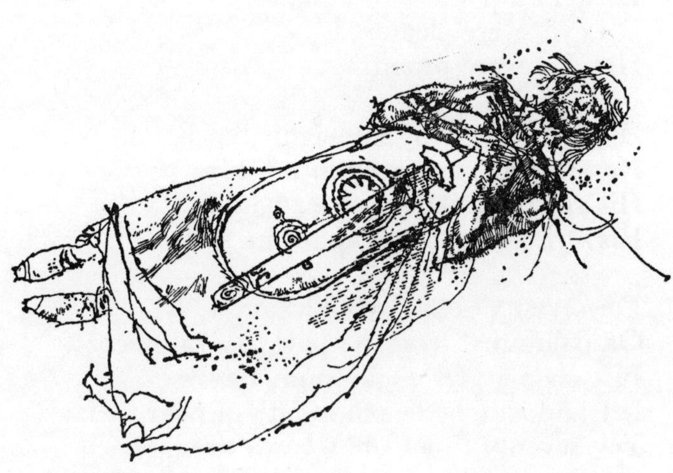

I Met an Old Man in the Lane

I met an old man in the lane;
His back was bent,
His head was bowed;
He held a pony by the mane;
His eyes were clear,
His eyes were proud.

He gripped me by my eight-year hand,
He gripped me by my lifted chin;
His grip was like a leather band,
His wrist was brown and thin.

'For seventy years I could have seen
On columned trees the pale, beech green;
Just once a year some sunny day
If I had watched each month of May;
Yes, seventy times—but I was tired,

Or busy with a this or that,
And six times in my life I stood
And throbbed with silence in the wood.'

He shook my chin in skinny hand,
He stared me in the eye,
His finger-pads rasped dry like sand,
He shook me with a cry.

'Look up, you little imp, look up.
You've got an ear, an eye.
Use them.
Who knows, a heron might
Beat grey across the sky.'

Aircraft Warning Light

Beyond the village and the farm
The pylons stride in Indian file,
And gaunt and lean below the stars
They cover silent mile on mile.

There is one fellow could be chief
That I can see when I'm in bed
Who waves the others on and holds
A blazing torch above his head.

He stands upon a little mound,
And proud and tall with narrowed eyes
He stares upon the distant line
Where seas heave up to touch the skies.

And when an aircraft homing low,
A wide-winged owl sweeps from the west,
His torch leans to the air-strip where
The rasping wheels can come to rest.

I crawl beneath the clothes and smile,
Float towards sleep as light as leaf;
The planes will all be guided home
By my unsleeping Indian chief.

The Dustbin Men

The older ones have gone to school,
My breakfast's on the plate,
But I can't leave the window-pane,
I might be just too late.

I've heard the clatter down the street,
I know they're creeping near,
The team of gruff-voiced, burly men
Who keep our dustbins clear.

And I must watch and see them clang
The dustbins on the road,
And stand in pairs to heave up high
The double-handled load.

Yes, there they come, the lorry growls
And grinds in bottom gear;
The dustman knees the garden gate
As, high up by his ear,
Firmly he balances the bin,
Head tilted to one side;
The great mouth of the rubbish cart
Is yawning very wide;
To me the mouth looks like a beast's,
A dragon's hungry jaws
That snap the refuse out of sight
Behind those sliding doors.

The lorry-dragon every day
Is in a ravenous mood,
And cardboard boxes, bottles, jars
Are all part of his food.

He gobbles up old magazines,
Saucepans and broken jugs,
Pieces of red linoleum,
And dirty, tufted rugs.

He crunches shattered pictures,
Old bicycles and tyres,
A bird-cage with its seed-tray,
Its bell and rusty wires;

And fractured clocks and mirrors,
A rocking-chair and broom,
A mattress and an iron bed;
Where does he find the room?

And like a dragon sated,
His great maw crammed quite tight,
He lifts his head and swallows
His breakfast out of sight.

What would the careless people
Who clutter up the street
Do without hungry dragons
To keep our houses neat?

Hay in Winter

The bullocks trample at the gate,
The tractor rumbles near,
Fred on the trailer forks the hay,
Winter is hard this year.
The grass is poor,
The ground is hard
Under the hooves
Like stable yard.
They toss their horns and jostle round;
High-tasselled tails on bony rumps
See-saw and bound;
The crescent curve of scattered hay
Pulls down the heads,
A rustling, dark,
Suddenly-ordered curve of beasts
Tethered by hunger in an arc.

The Coach

I never really saw
The coach and horses on the moor;
I never saw them in the lane
With flying tail and lifting mane;
But where the lines of beeches curve
And make an avenue of green
I heard,
I heard the things unseen.
While cowering in the roadside grass
I heard the gentry proudly pass,
And with my knuckles in my teeth
I waited till they rolled beneath
The arching branches of the trees.

The whirring spokes spun past my knees.
I heard the snorting nostrils blow,
The slap of reins,
The jingling bit,
The high coach tilt on squeaking spring,

24

The squelch of mud,
The sudden ring
Of iron tyre upon a stone.
I heard the swearing coachman lurch
Into the slope beside the church.
Then silence soft and dark.

And when they'd gone I ran my hand
Across that ancient grassy track;
The half-moons scooped by pounding hoof,
Indented, narrow ruts of wheels—
Here in my finger-tips the proof
Of things you dare not say have been.

And in the morning sun no sign,
No scooped-out turf,
No curving slots;
Nothing to see by light of day
That coach and pair had passed this way.

Yellow Cat

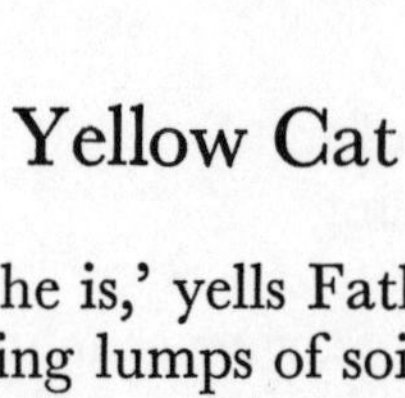

'There he is,' yells Father,
Grabbing lumps of soil,
'That yellow tabby's on the fence.
Drown him in boiling oil.
He's scratching at my runner beans.
Bang at the window, quick.
Wait till I get my laces done
I'll beat him with my stick.'

'Too late,' they shout, 'he's on the fence.
He's turning, Father, wait.'

'I'll give him turning, I'll be there,
I'll serve him on a plate.'

They banged the window, Father stormed
And hopped with wild despair;
The cat grew fat with insolence
And froze into a stare.
Its brazen glare stopped Father
With its blazing yellow light;
The silken shape turned slowly
And dropped gently out of sight.

The Weathercock

From cold and windy perch the cock
Looks down the steeple's cliff of slates
And over grey and sleeping town
Impatiently for daybreak waits.

Cry, 'Cock a rock a rock a roo',
And wake the grocer and the clerk;
Cry, 'Cock a rock a rock a roo',
And get the yawning dogs to bark.

The sun is elbowing its way
Over the rough slope of the hill,
And with its yellow light it shines
On church and cottage, shop and mill.

Cry, 'Cock a rock a rock a roo'—
To join you where you twirl and glare—
Cry, 'Cock a rock a rock a roo'—
Only a steeplejack would dare.

You close your lids to winter storms,
You thrust into the wind your beak,
You answer with a grating squawk
The gull's defiant, wind-thrown shriek.

Cry, 'Cock a roo', cry high and shrill;
Must you be brought down for repair?
You lie so huge but strangely still
Stretched lifeless on the pavement there.

Helicopter

Heli, Heli, Heli
Copter,
Miss Brown was strolling when it stopped
    her;
Very, very nearly dropped her
Shopping-bag in sudden fright
At the monstrous clatter-flight.
All the men lean on their spades
And watch the flashing rotor-blades.
Gavin (watches television plays)
Yelled, 'Look, a coastal rescue chopper—
Most exciting thing for days—
Isn't it a yellow whopper?'
Like a maddened bumble-bee
It has him twisting round to see;
Makes all the village heads corkscrew

To wave a welcome to the crew,
Who nonchalant through open door
Wave as they squat upon the floor.
Gavin (and all the racing boys)
Rejoices in the noose of noise;
But stern Miss Brown now flushed with rage
Is scribbling a double page.
'Write to the paper, yes, I must;
I shall express my deep disgust.'
While in a near-by field the sheep,
A woolly, lumpy, startled heap,
Bolted,
Halted,
Cropped a
Little faster,
Bewildered by the helicopter.

The Forest

So thick and close the forest trees
That as I lie and stare
I can see only trunks and stems
And branches everywhere.

Mile upon mile the greenish gloom,
Frightening and immense,
Masses with undergrowth and bush
Impenetrably dense.

No sky above the trees is seen,
No path before me lies,
The fierce beasts crouching for attack
Follow me with their eyes.

And often when the darkness comes
And wraps the traveller round,
He wanders blundering through the trees
And nevermore is found.

This is no place to be alone
With fearful, turning head;
In the black silence of the night
I'd rather be in bed.

And there is mother calling.
How soon the minutes pass
When you are peering cheek to ground
Through forest's meadow grass.

I stand and round my ankles
The forest sighs and sways,
Mile upon mile of meadow's
Shimmering grassy haze.

I'll tell them of my journey;
The months in lonely camps;
Forced marches in the darkness
With smoky, swinging lamps;

Of ants as big as tigers—
'Yes, Mother, coming soon'—
I'll come back to my forest
Tomorrow afternoon.

Australian Visitor

I went to London recently
And took a 9a bus,
And found that I was seated by
A duck-billed platypus.

Of course, there's nothing odd or strange
About this slight event,
But I admit I was intrigued
To see which way he went.

He held a sticky ten-pence coin
Flat on his skin-webbed hand,
And with antipodean voice
Asked clearly for the Strand.

I knew then by his accent,
I knew and I was right,
He'd get off at Australia House
And sleep there for the night.

I said to him, 'Nice evening';
He turned his flattened jaws;
He made as if to answer me
And offered me his paws.

A double-handed handshake,
I thought, is rather grand;
He just had time to say, 'Indeed,'
When someone shouted, 'Strand.'

It's hard to get off quickly
When your legs are rather short,
And I had a sudden panic
When his poison spur got caught.

It was tucked inside my pocket—
Could it really kill a man?—
But he freed it with his five strong nails
And shuffled down and ran.

He ran along the centre aisle
And stepped into the street;
A cycle following behind
Just missed his little feet.

'Goodbye,' I shouted, 'and Good Luck.'
I wish there had been time
To talk of Platypus affairs
In Platypussian mime.

Passengers stared through windows
And made a dreadful fuss,
And all because they'd travelled with
A duck-billed platypus.

They gazed at me and whispered,
'I'm sure. Whatever next!'
Until their silly chattering
Stirred me till I was vexed.

The driver gaped with open mouth,
Then turned to look at me;
'I say. That something from a zoo
That's just got blinking free?'

I rose with dignity and said,
'You all are most unkind.
That was a most distinguished—er—man
That you have left behind.

'Of course he's rather primitive,
His family's very old;
How rude to stare and spy upon
A stranger in the cold.

'Are you "Monotremata"?'
They shrank before my frown.
'No, I suppose your family tree
Is Smith or Jones or Brown.'

The bus had stopped, they turned and
        looked,
Their eyes were opened wide;
Outside Australia House he bowed
And disappeared inside.

At a Bear-baiting

Suddenly before my wheels
Lurches an unexpected hare,
And only glassy eyes reveal
The terror stabbing everywhere.

An empty track, fields either side,
No wire or fence to hold it in;
The creature tethered to the road,
Flayed by the engine's revving din.

The menace of the hunter's size,
The beat of hammers on the brain;
A touch of throttle cuffs it back
Into the tunnel of the lane.

I tap the measure for its leap,
I pipe for its ungainly dance;
With cruel pressure of my toe
I conjure its obsessive prance.

I stop the car and with a nod
Release to grass the shivering hare,
And through its rolling eye I ask
Some natural dignity to share.

It see-saws through the stubble field,
By beech-trees on the crest is framed,
And as it leaves the circus tent
I have the grace to feel ashamed.

Alone in the Grange

Strange,
Strange,
Is the little old man
Who lives in the Grange.
Old,
Old;
And they say that he keeps
A box full of gold.
Bowed,
Bowed,
Is his thin little back
That once was so proud.
Soft,
Soft,
Are his steps as he climbs
The stairs to the loft.
Black,
Black,
Is the old shuttered house.
Does he sleep on a sack?

They say he does magic,
That he can cast spells,
That he prowls round the garden
Listening for bells;
That he watches for strangers,
Hates every soul,
And peers with his dark eye
Through the keyhole.

I wonder, I wonder,
As I lie in my bed,
Whether he sleeps with his hat on his head?
Is he really magician
With altar of stone,
Or a lonely old gentleman
Left on his own?

Miss Torrent

Little Miss Torrent drives a car.
Nothing surprising in that?
You'd think there was if you saw her ride by
Resplendent in flowery hat;
For little Miss Torrent,
Hunched over the wheel,
Scares everybody in town;
When people see her rushing along
They're sure she will batter them down.
They squirm as she crashes the gears and screams
With a stab of the brake to a stop;
They cover their faces to shut out the sight
As she spins on the ice like a top.
They daren't use the crossing
For fear she is blind
To the lollipop man with his stick;
As she squeezes the kerb with a squeal of her tyres
Pedestrians feel dizzy and sick.
But when you are driving yourself it is worst
For she scorches the old village street
As if she were driving a rallying car
With a champion racer to beat.
And by far worst of all are the deep narrow lanes
If you happen to see her approach,
For the lane is suddenly as dangerous as if
You were meeting a six-wheeler coach;
For she rarely pays heed to the motorist's code
And invariably drives the wrong side of the road.

Pony and Trap

Two men,
Fat,
Sat
One in a cap,
One in a sweat-stained, trilby hat,
In a small round trap;
Reins dry, cracked and flat
Lay
Across one thick-thighed lap.
But a trap
With the smell of leather,
And pony.
How can you drop
On a main road
On the clip, clip, clop
Of a small black pony
With a trap
And two men,
Fat,
Unaware of traffic roar,
Doing a delicate, trap see-saw
On the wheels.

If two round
Fat men lean back
They lift a pony off the ground;
If they lurch forward to the breeze
They squeeze a pony to his knees.
A trap
On a road
Today,

Towed
By a black pony—
And two men
Laughing and nodding now and then,
Followed by a load
Of hay,
Coaches tearing the air away
Like calico,
Motors rasping along the road,
Then fuming behind at having to stop
For the unheeding, jogging clippety-clop
Of a pony
Pulling a trap
With two fat men,
One in a cap.

Racing the Train

A train, a train;
Turn round quick in the end of the lane;
The roads are quiet, do you think we could
Take the short cut through the wood,
And slice between the oats and corn
To catch the diesel's warning horn.

There is the valley; by the wood
We scrambled from the car and stood.
The signal's down, the crossing's clear,
The throbbing carriages are near;
And from the forest's dim, green light
The curving train thrusts into sight.

How strange to watch a train and feel
A goodness that had power to heal;
For virtue we could not explain
Shone round that boy beside the lane,
And blessed that moment and that place
With its immeasurable grace.

The Night of the Wild Horses

Come to the window;
See the fair sprawled asleep,
Each caravan and trailer,
Stall and roundabout a heap
Humped in the moonlight
On the village green.

Put on a scarf and coat
And climb over the sill;
Now run between
The loaded apple-trees.
The fruit
Thumps in the shadow circle
On the ground.
In heavy-lidded sleep
Vans rest in mist high
As the axles.
Not a sound
Except the lift and sigh
Of breath.

Come to the horses
For they do not sleep,
But, tense and watchful,
Ready for mounting keep
Nostril to tail, tethered but free,
Their silvered immobility.
Cob, hunter, skewbald, bay,
Shetland and piebald,

Dappled grey—
Along their bristly manes
We ran our hands;
They whinnied to the leafy lanes.
They chewed the bits,
Their teeth were bared,
The lifted, reddened nostrils flared;
Each sleek, proud head
Turned,
And as the sleepers moaned in bed
The horses with impatience burned.

We chose,
Scrambled a varnished back;
The wooden, creaking muscles strained;
We heard the iron brackets crack
And from the silent roundabout
We leapt and rode with muffled shout.
And as we galloped thigh to thigh
The stars hissed past us in the sky.

Along the moonlit lanes we sped
With lifted head by straining head,
And desperately leaned to squeeze
The living strength between our knees.
Through pools of light, through patch of shade
We speared that clattering cavalcade;
And by the pack-horse bridge we leapt
Wave after wave the hawthorn hedge,
Splashed through a hollow spiked with sedge,
Left far behind the road
And swept,

A fluid shape that seemed to soar,
Up to the foothills of the moor;
The iron clap of hoof on road
Was quickly deadened as we strode;
Flank glistening by sweaty flank
We drummed and thumped the grassy bank;
We felt the cold air rush and flow
Into the valley cleft below.

With stirrups gone
We clawed
The manes wiry and coarse and black;
The hooves thundered along the moorland track;
We pressed our cheeks against the slide
Of hot necks
Where the sleek, wet hide
Tightened with every lengthened stride;
In every lifted, puckered fold
The bunching muscle coiled and rolled;
The nostrils, belled with cold, stretched wide
To power this mad, explosive ride.

Uphill the reach of hooves dug hard;
The quarters
Gathered for the thrust
And slammed the drier slopes to dust.
The tight-packed troop
Jostled and muzzled,
And the wind blew clean
The gaping jaws foam-frothed with green.
We clung and gripped
While twenty panting creatures ripped
A swathe of dark earth as they pressed
Up to the hill-fort on the crest.

The tribesmen peered above the ditch,
The rampart fences throbbed with fear;
The pebble nestled in the sling,
And arrows notched the tautened string;
Rough fingers weighed a spear or sword
And waited for the misty horde.
And now the gateway threatened large
Our violently reckless charge.

We had no power to control
The heaving, jolting thrusting troop;
In every jaw teeth wide and bare
Snorted and snaffled at the air;
The tails and manes streamed back like rags,
Torn, lifted, wind-split flags;
And stones flung low from heels
Rattled on boulders far away
With ring of flinty ricochet.

Some signal to the warriors came;
No missiles flew,
No shout arose;
But ponderously the fortress gate
Creaked wide
And gave us passage from outside;
Our gallop slowed,
And we with jogging canter rode
Through rampart twists,
Through glinting spears,
Up the wood-barred earthen ramp
Into the last ditch of the camp.

Ahead the dotted camp-fires glowed;
Fierce warriors in the red light strode;
With warlike stance
They watched our tentative advance.
Behind us riderless
Without command
The troop of horses wheeled and fanned
Into the inmost ditch.
The leaders raced,
The hindmost found their place and paced

With gentle trot
Until the line was lengthened out
Into a natural roundabout.
Nostril to tail, the rhythm caught,
They made their circle round the fort.

And we rode on,
Still side by side.
The gathering tribesmen parted wide;
Our horses shivered in the weird
Silence,
Whinnied and on their haunches reared,
Then moved again across the ground
To halt before the central mound.

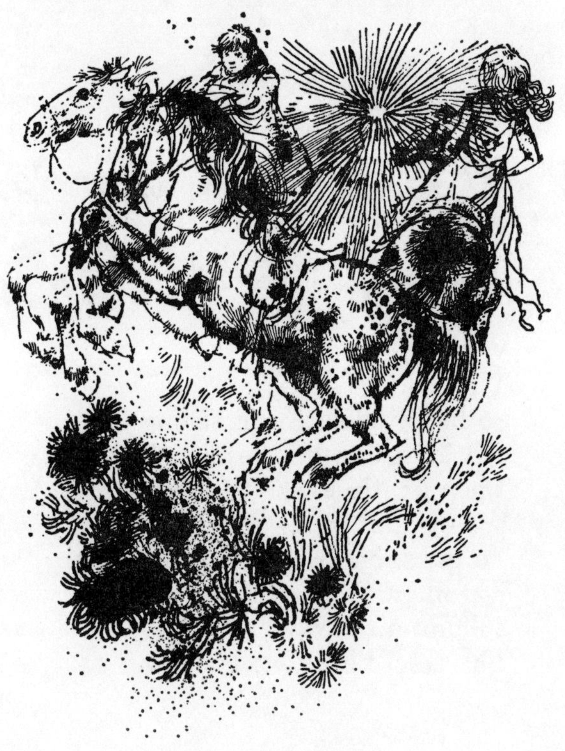

High on a platform lean, severe,
The chieftain sat.
The warriors roared,
Excited by the circling beasts
And by the strangers moving near
To bow before their noble lord.
The old man rose;
We had no fear
When he an iron sword raised high;
There was compassion in his eye
Which, grey and clear,
Looked on us as his guests not foes.

We bowed our heads;
The heavy sword,
So lightly held in his strong hand,
Circled us with a flashing band,
Then gently lowered.
We did not dare
To question as it touched our hair,
For silent there,
Solemn and grave,
The chief his ancient blessing gave.

He briefly spoke—
'Peace in your hearts;
Do not forget, you must return;
You now are joined by magic art.'
A pale fire flared
And in his eyes began to burn.

We clutched the reins,
Our horses reared,
Whinnied and circled in the dust;
We waved farewell
And threw our weight
Into the gallop for the gate.

The horses prancing in the ditch,
Sensing our lead,
Swept with a sudden surge of speed,
Followed in file
And plunged into the downhill mile.
Against the sky
The rushing string of horses ran,
An undulating caravan
Which broke and rose and lunged and fell

On boulder, hummock, rocky ledge,
Squelched through the swamp
And crushed the sedge
Right to the plain
Where smooth was laid
The flat and curving river-blade.
And there by pack-horse bridge the troop
Slithered and reared into a group,
Nostril to centre trembling there;
Each mouth-cloud joined
And in the air
Hung grey like smoke.

We drew aside but neither spoke;
We watched the horses swerve and kick,
And lift their wildly rolling eyes
Up to the moon-shot, leaden skies.
They shuffled back
Crowding us to the centre,
And from the opened circle bowed
Their heads:
Inside the ring
Mounted we stood alone,
Carved in a slaty moonlit stone,
And neither stirred,
For eyes compulsively alert
Hiding some mute and struggling hurt
Had little need
Of uttering a single word.

Who rode with me?—
A slender child
With long, pale features and a wild
Beauty in the free
Fall of her hair
And the bare grace of her limbs;
Her eyes were dark,
Proud was her voice,
And I was fearful for this time
Was the tense moment of her choice.

'Ride back, ride back to the wild hill-side;
Gallop back to the wide
Arc of heathered moor;
Sit with me on the earthen floor
Of hill-fort hut;
Remember the iron sword.'

But her eyes were cold and she was young;
She wheeled and the circled beasts were flung
Apart to let her go.
I heeled my horse and clutched her rein,
But she jerked the leather free again.

'Ride back, ride back.'
But the clip and clopper like a pain
Scattered my thoughts about the lane;
The closeness of that stolen ride,
The tenderness I had to hide,
The heat inside that diamond frost
Were now irrevocably lost.

In a grey sleep the village green . . .
We walked our horses in between
The vans and stalls;
Shadows like thick wool shawls
Draped every corner.
In a strange quiet we stepped
Towards the roundabout.
Softly the horses leapt
To their own places,
Kept
Unsteadily a balance and were still,
Hooves lifted, knees neatly bent
Under the striped cone of the tent.
Who would have said
That we had ever left our bed?
Only our mud-encrusted clothes,
The miry bellies, necks sweat-lined,
The clods of earth beneath each horse
For puzzled fairground hand to find.

She walked ahead and closed a door;
And from the hills it seemed a roar
Of anger rolled.
Over the skyline dark and bare
A giant sword flashed in the air.

It was so long ago, of course . . .
I only walk now with my horse,
And let him muzzle down and snort
At thin grass in an empty fort.
Magic like that is never caught
So easily when you are old;
But sometimes in the autumn cold
There comes a time
When I pretend
That, as I pick a careful climb
To where the gateway opens wide,
My love still gallops at my side.

One thing I know is not pretence—
This windy hill throbs with a sense
Of wonder;
Bare, barren with the ramparts honed
To softer edges it is loaned
To us only;
Sometimes I almost see immense
Throngs of defenders;
Almost touch the mighty blade
That on our heads was gently laid.

I don't pretend about my horse.
I have to heel and use the stick,
I have to drive with all my force
To urge him through the ditch;
His ears lie back, his nostrils twitch,
And white and wild his rolling eye—

Yet there is nothing.
The puckered ramparts empty lie
Skimmed by the wind.

I pulled him once on foot;
Pawing the ground
He inched towards the chieftain's central mound—
But not again . . .
He reared and screamed
And dragged me right across the fort
Through the defensive ring;
A furlong gone before I brought
His terror to a halt.
I smelt the steaming, sweaty salt
Of his exhausted shivering,
And talked him down the moorland ride
Hobbling and stumbling by his side.

Still as a coat thrown down the hill-fort lay;
A dipping curlew beat its way
Over the wrinkled hill;
Darkness began to spill
Into the valley;
I mounted with a groan and slow
We nodded on.
That other ride?
It was so long ago.